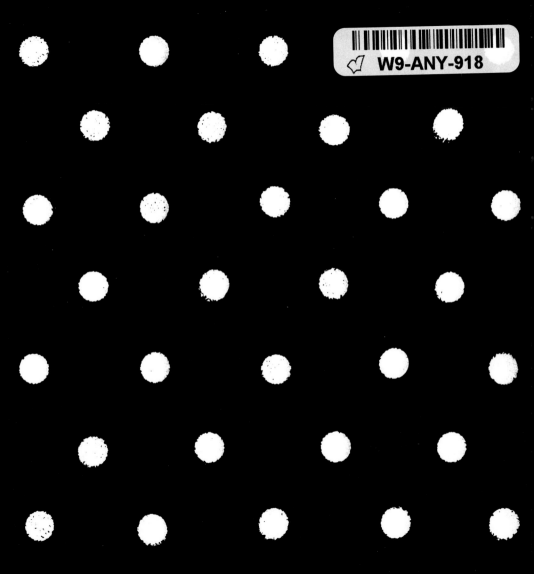

W9-ANY-918

If It's Not About Me, I'm Busy

Pearl's Guide to Living Large and Having A Stunning Shoe Wardrobe

Eric Scott

**Andrews McMeel
Publishing**

Kansas City

If It's Not About Me, I'm Busy:
Pearl's Guide to Living Large and Having
A Stunning Shoe Wardrobe

ISBN: 0-7407-5096-8

05 06 07 08 09 WKT 10 9 8 7 6 5 4 3 2 1

Written and illustrated by Eric Scott

Library of Congress Control Number: 2004111536

If It's Not About Me, I'm Busy

Shopping, snacking, napping—life can be a rich and rewarding experience when you take center stage and fully embrace what is <u>really</u> important. Of course there are other compelling activities competing for your attention—watching that cold front come through on the weather channel, finding and buying every color of a really comfortable shoe, and making it through at least 24 hours without saying, "What is <u>wrong</u> with you?" to someone. My point is, whatever you do in life, do it in a big way. Do it large. Super-size that attitude. You can't overdo it, because it's all about <u>you</u>.

So enjoy!

Don't be fooled by low-fat diets. The real reason they're called low-fat diets is because the nanosecond you go off these diets, the <u>low</u> parts of your body will receive all the <u>fat</u> you thought you'd lost.

Take command of the remote and treat yourself to a full evening of your favorite entertainment.

Don't let stress get in the way of your daily routine. Take it out on anyone near you and you'll feel energized and refreshed.

Don't let getting older slow you down.
You can absolutely, most definitely,
still make the bar scene.

Give in to reality. There comes a time when our hips and thighs form a very powerful club whose mission statement is, "To keep the club large, and maybe even grow it larger."

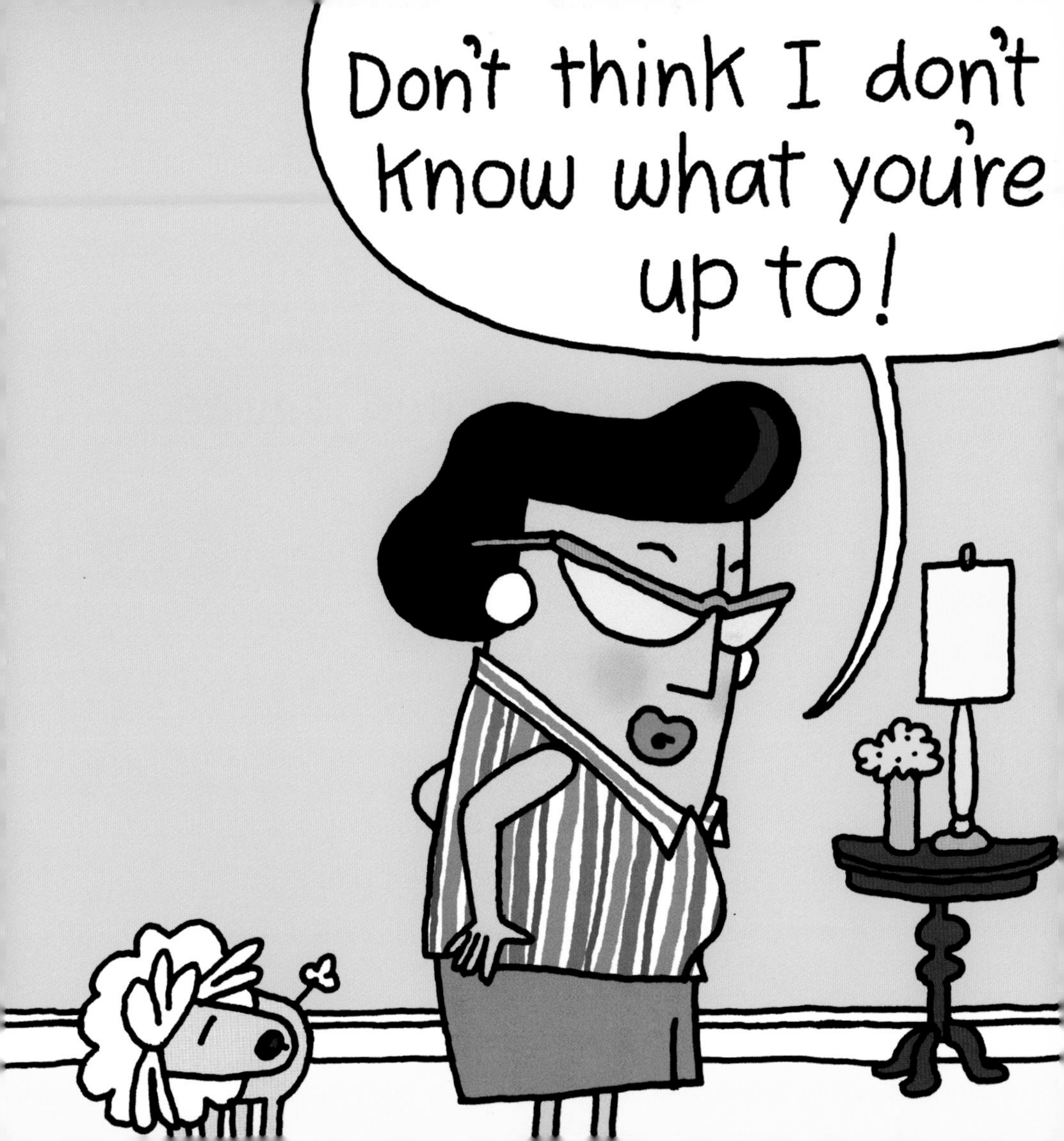
Don't think I don't Know what you're up to!

Dole out unsolicited advice.

Continue to expand your shoe collection. Most experts agree that owning several hundred pairs of shoes can get rid of depression and some skin rashes.

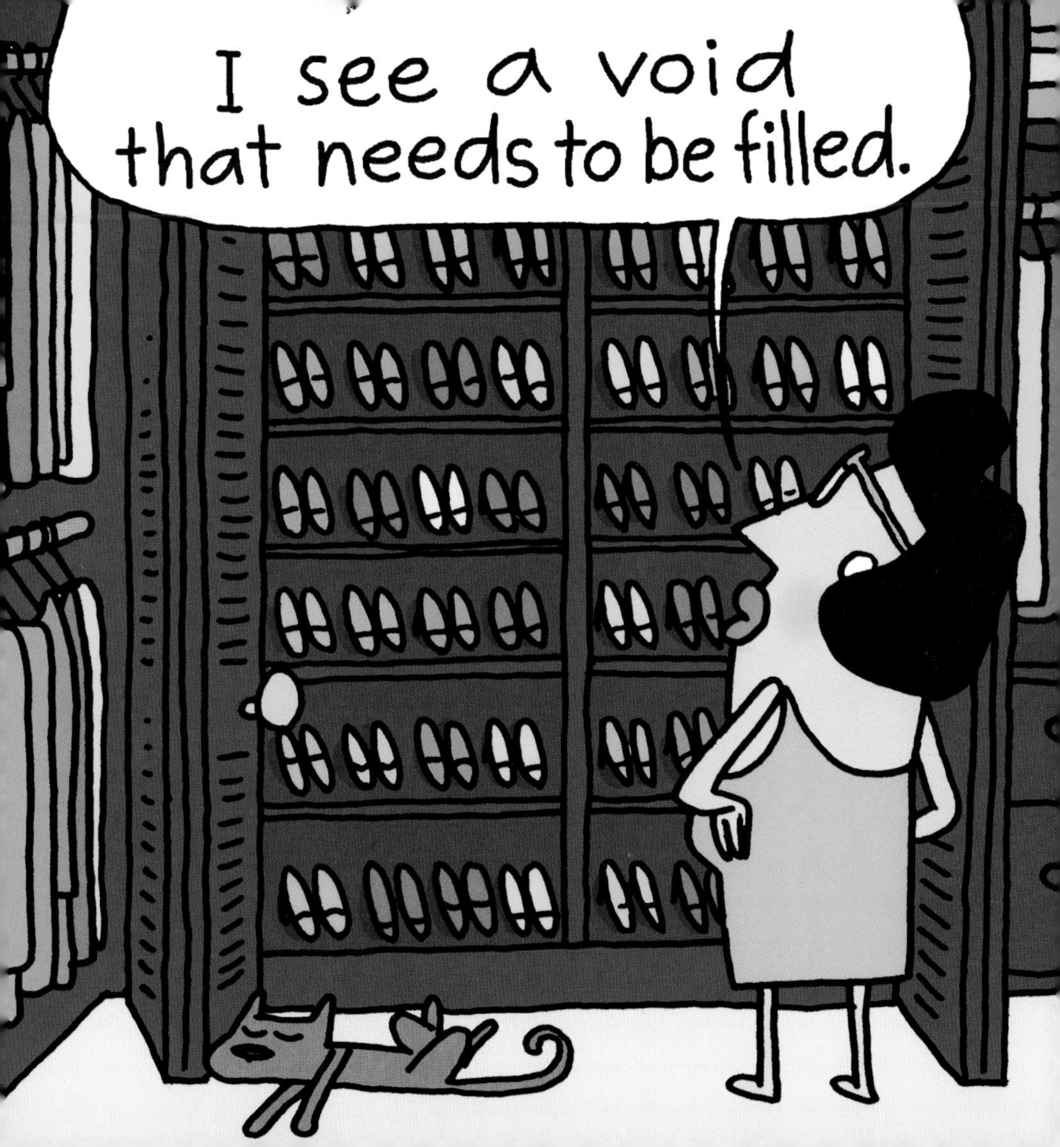
I see a void that needs to be filled.

Create a fresh approach to
your daily "to-do" list.

Find new ways to communicate with your husband. Using words like "cheeseburger," "hammer" or "nail gun" to get his attention can bring about an alertness that is not unlike what you see at the Westminster Dog show — though he won't be as well-groomed.

Do a little thinking outside the box the next time you experience hot flashes.

Find a mantra that suits your needs and then meditate.

Choose your favorite activity and make it a daily thing.

Find ways to better understand your husband. Spend some time with his best friend.

Eat right by maintaining a year-round healthful diet and indulge only during the holidays.

Volunteer for babysitting duty. You will create a lifetime of memories for the little ones.

Keep a daily journal. It can help enhance your life, make you a better person and lead to self-discovery.

Support the arts.

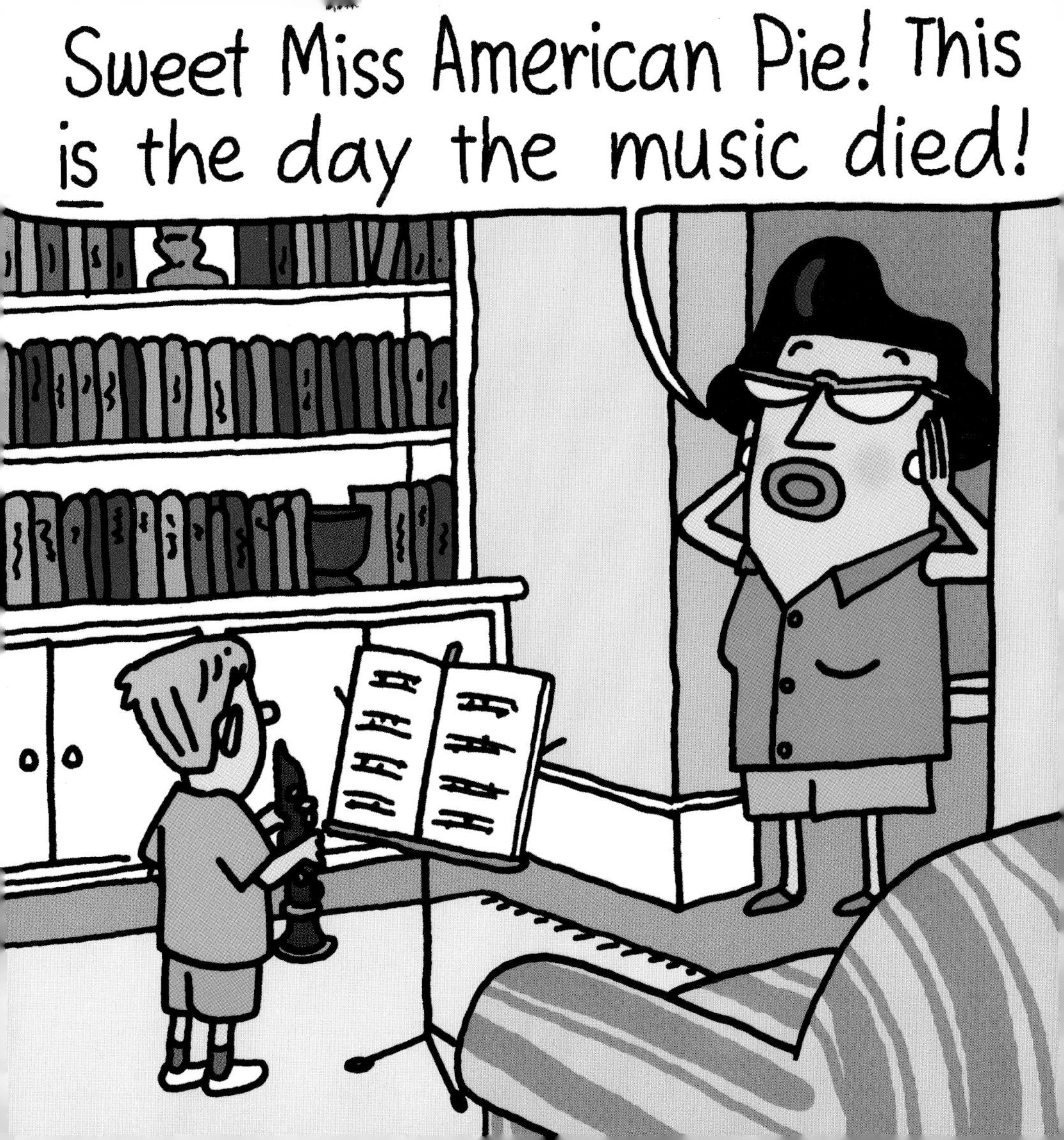
Sweet Miss American Pie! This is the day the music died!

As you get older, you should continue to exercise.

Conquer your weakness for little rich chocolatey things by turning it into a hobby. Then, indulging yourself becomes "pursuing your interest."

Get a pet. They can be faithful companions, bringing years of emotional support, constant entertainment, and enough fur to create "little accents" throughout your home.

Indulge young minds.

Okay, I give up! What's scarier than a Wicked Witch and... and...
wet all over!
...wet all over?

Face up to certain truths—flinging your underwear at a rock star on stage is no longer an option.

Find creative ways to conserve energy.

Vary your daily snack times. Late night snacking can be a lot more fun than daytime snacking.

Acknowledge that forgetting why you entered a room in the first place is just part of the whole natural aging process thing.

It's important to maintain a fitness goal.

Keep everyone in their place.

Nurture your inner green thumb that yearns to express itself.

Find a support group when going through the "big change."

Well, guess that's all the tips for now. Hope you enjoyed them.

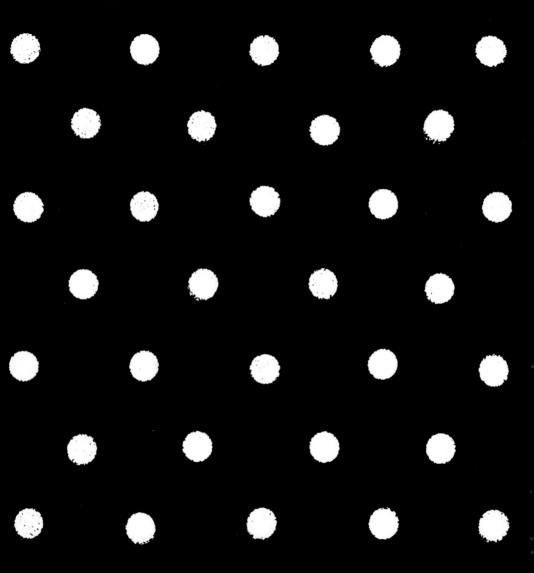